Pray Like a Son

NEIL KENNEDY

Contents

1

Pray Like a Son

"I tell you the truth, unless you turn from your sins and become like little children, you will never get into the Kingdom of Heaven. So anyone who becomes as humble as this little child is the greatest in the Kingdom of Heaven." - Jesus

> Principle: Jesus redefined what it means to be in a relationship with God as a son.

I wanted to name this book, Pray Like a Man. However, as I began to study, meditate, and ask the Holy Spirit what to write and convey on prayer, I felt strongly to look at the pattern of how Jesus prayed.

Jesus prayed like no one before Him. Jesus approached God, the Holy One of Israel, saying, *"Father...."*

This approach to prayer is a radical shift in the concept of praying. So much so that the Pharisees accused Jesus of blasphemy by calling Yahweh as His own Father. By replacing the Hebrew name of God, revealed to Moses, with the honorific but the very personal moniker of Father, Jesus was emphasizing his identity.

Another hesitation in entitling this teaching, *Pray Like a Son*, was because I know men. Men do not want to be childish. We find the notion of being a child again, silly at best, more likely, repulsive. So, to suggest that we should identify ourselves in the humble position of a child is a tough sell in a culture of "Man Up."

Even Rabbi Nicodemus questioned the notion of returning as a child when Jesus told him that he must be "born again."

> *"How can someone be born when they are old?" Nicodemus asked. "Surely they cannot enter a second time into their mother's womb to be born!" – John 3:4*

Yet, I would also argue that most of us want our prayers to be heard, received, and returned in the affirmative. And, can we expect to be heard if we approach God in the same way that He approached God, namely, in the position of a son. I would also point out that no one had a better grasp than having His prayers heard than Jesus. So, He is our model of prayer.

I was not raised a Christian. I was a heathen. Alcoholism, drug addiction, and adultery were the norm in our household. As quickly as I graduated high school, I left home, hoping for a better life but lacking mentorship or parental leadership to direct my path proved to be too much for my naivety.

I worked in a strip coal mine in southeastern Oklahoma. I worked 12 hours a day, seven nights a week, from 7 pm to 7 am. My job was to pump water out of the mine into a retention pond.

It was hard. I worked at the mine alone.

My life was already a mess. I was lost. I was depressed. I was on the verge of destruction.

As I looked up into the sky, seeing the stars at night, assuming that God was up there and nowhere near me, I exclaimed, "God, do you know me? Do you care?"

It was the first time that I heard the Voice of God; yes, I heard Him. Audibly? Maybe. I don't know if the verbal vibrations of His Voice were public or private or spoken only to my spirit. But I know who I heard. My ears heard God say directly to me.

If any man has ears to hear, let him hear. - Mark 4:23

He said to me, *"Yes, I know you. I know your name. I have given you the spirit of a son so that you may call me, Abba, Father."*

Before that night, I had never read scripture, so you can imagine my surprise and confirmation when I read Romans 8:15, *"The Spirit you received does not make you slaves so that you live in fear again; rather, the Spirit you received brought about your adoption to sonship. And by Him, we cry, "Abba, Father."*

For me, this experience was as powerful as Saul's experience on the road to Damascus.

Unlike me, Saul was not a heathen, **"he was circumcised the eighth day, of the stock of Israel, the tribe of Benjamin, a Hebrew of Hebrews; concerning the Law, a Pharisee; concerning zeal, persecuting the Church; concerning the righteousness which is in the Law, blameless."** (Philippians 3:4-8)

Yet, Saul's relationship with God was not intimate because he related to God only through his credentialing until the

Christophany (the appearance or manifestation of Christ by Light). Saul's idea of religious merit was proving oneself, disciplining himself to holiness, serving, sacrificing, and yes, even persecuting people who thought they knew God intimately through Jesus of Nazareth.

Unfortunately, this kind of god-service is widespread in religions, even Christianity. It is remarkable how many raised eyebrows, smirks, and scoffing you will see when you begin to identify yourself as a son of God.

> Principle: The position of merit for prayer is not credentials, works, sacrifices, or rituals; it is a relationship.

Men are very uncomfortable with the proximity that calling God, Father, makes them. Men want a God, but they either want to serve him from a distance or confine him into a manageable trinket.

Some men want God to keep distant so that they don't have to deal with His presence and the ramifications of seeing His holiness.

> *When the people heard the thunder and the loud blast of the ram's horn, and when they saw the flashes of lightning and the smoke billowing from the mountain, they stood at a distance, trembling with fear.*
>
> *And they said to Moses, "You speak to us, and we will listen. But don't let God speak directly to us, or we will die!" — Exodus 20:18-19*

Other men want God to fit in their pockets or on the mantle. They may want to light candles and bow on their cushy rugs.

> *"What good is an idol carved by man,*
>   *or a cast image that deceives you?*
>   *How foolish to trust in your own creation—*
>   *a god that can't even talk!*
>   *What sorrow awaits you who say to wooden idols,*
>   *'Wake up and save us!'*
>   *To speechless stone images you say,*
>   *'Rise up and teach us!'*
>   *Can an idol tell you what to do?*
>   *They may be overlaid with gold and silver,*
>   *but they are lifeless inside.*
>   *But the Lord is in his holy Temple.*
>   *Let all the earth be silent before him."* - Habakkuk 2:18-20

God's relationship with Man started with walks in the Garden. Of course, the embezzlement of Adam cost him that communion with God. Later in this book, I want to give you the seven steps to turn your daily commute into communion. But for now, I hope you grasp the profound change in position of prayer that Jesus introduced by referring to God as Father. So much so that He was accused of blasphemy for saying it.

> *Jesus replied, "My Father is always working, and so am I." So the Jewish leaders tried all the harder to find a way to kill him. For he not only broke the Sabbath, but he also called God his Father, thereby making himself equal with God.* —John 5:17

5

Most religions do not have the concept of God being a Father. They much rather live in fear and be a slave than have the responsibility, freedom, and burden of Divine heritage.

When Jesus appeared to Saul, He said, "Why are you persecuting me?"

Saul was persecuting the Church. Jesus was dead to him. Saul was only trying to stamp out the growing movement of Christ-followers or The Way as they were being known. The reason that the early Christians were called, The Way is a reference that Jesus said that we would have access to the Father through Him when He said, "I am the Way, the Truth, and the Life. No one comes to the Father except through me." (John 14:6)

Stopping The Way was the perfect mission for the zealous Saul to prove his unwavering devotion to serving God, even to the point of imprisoning or killing these blasphemers.

> "They will put you out of the synagogue; in fact, the time is coming when anyone who kills you will think they are offering a service to God." - John 16:2

Principle: It's hard to rationalize with someone willing to kill another person for their god.

That may be why Christ personally appeared to Saul on that road. No one could have stood against the credentials of Saul to persuade him to see Christ. So, Christ appeared and then blinded him so that Saul could perceive spiritually and see Jesus.

Saul does convert to Christ, confessing Jesus as Lord, and becoming a true son of Abraham, through faith, not by observing the Law, not by the circumcision of his manhood, but by renting his heart and believing in the Lordship and substitutionary atonement of Christ.

But whom am I to hear God speak to me as a Father speaks to a son?

I don't have credentials for pedigree. I have no heritage. I am not of Abraham's seed. Yet, I heard the Voice say to me, *"You can call me, Abba, Father."*

I wasn't religious enough to know how radical that concept would be and how Biblical it is to speak directly to God and call Him Father.

This experience has given me an assurance that is not based on what I have done or can do but on who I am. I have absolute confidence that I am a son of God. Again, don't allow religious sensitivities to disturb you by saying this. I didn't say that I am *the* Son of God. I said, "I am *a* son of God." All I knew was that I heard the Voice of God and wanted to keep hearing Him.

This experience laid a foundation for my faith, an unwavering belief that my identity in Christ is assured in sonship.

A few years ago, my adult children had all read the book *Strength Finders* by Tom Rath. The book also has a personality test to discover your strengths. My children were very interested in learning what my strengths are. They were completely surprised when my number one strength was self-assurance. When discussing the results, I pointed out that the test was misreading me. I asserted that my assurance had nothing to do with me but was reading my absolute certainty of who I am in Christ. I have no confidence in my flesh, but Christ is my assurance.

7

You Can Call Me, Abba

Because you are his sons, God sent the Spirit of his Son
into our hearts, the Spirit who calls out, "Abba, Father."
– Galatians 4:6

When God changed Saul's name to Paul, He did so as a Father has the right to name His son. Paul opened his eyes to sonship by telling the Galatians Church, *"You are his sons."*

Abba means Father. It has the more endearing sense of saying, Daddy or Papa.

To be transparent, you may find it very difficult to begin your prayer time with this endearing term, approaching God by saying, "Daddy" or "Papa" or even "Father."

You may also hear the accusatory murmurings of the Pharisees when you do it. I've listened to them also,

"Who are you?"

"Who do you think that you are?

"How dare you approach God this way!"

Yet, when Jesus introduced prayer, He taught us to approach God by saying, "Our Father in heaven, may your name be kept holy."

> Principle: Jesus is saying that by calling God, Abba, Father, we recognize His holiness, not dismissing it by associating ourselves with Him.

This teaching is to help you position yourself in the identity of sonship so that you can pray to your Father and be heard. By the conclusion of this teaching, I hope you radically change your position to step up to sonship and pray like a son.

> **Action Step:** Drop me a note and tell me the experience you have after praying this way for the first time. Please email me at NeilKennedy@FivestarMan.com.

2

This is How You Are To Pray

Once Jesus was in a certain place praying. As he finished, one of his disciples came to him and said, "Lord, teach us to pray, just as John taught his disciples." - Luke 11:1

The pattern and persistence of Jesus' prayer life distinguished his prayers so much that the disciples wanted to know how to pray. Each disciple would have been very accustomed to the Jewish faith's rituals, traditions, and routines as Jewish children. These rites remind people to be grateful for God's deliverance in the past and position them for the prophecies of their future.

However, there was something more present in the prayer life of Jesus. He was the promised Deliverer, and He fulfills the prophecies. So, His presence was current. He was fulfilling His assignment as the Son of Man on the earth. In other words, He was and always is present.

The distinction of the way Jesus prayed was that it seemed so personal, not religious. It wasn't ceremonial; even when he was fulfilling the rites of the Jewish faith, the intimacy of his relationship with his Father was so evident and captivating. Jesus took things that were shadows and enlightened them. He took blurred images of feasts, copies if you will, and made them original. *He* was what everything pointed to fulfill.

> Principle: You will never fulfill your purpose on earth
> if you do not commune (spiritually communicate) with
> the Creator of it.

It's so interesting that Jesus, who was with the Father in eternity and came from the Father into the realm of time and captivated by space, would withdraw from everyone to seek solitude to be with the Father.

Think of it. Jesus only had a short time in the flesh to be with humanity, yet, he would withdraw from everyone to be with the Father — their relationship was so close, so connected that He prayed constantly.

After seeing this pattern, one of the disciples asked him to teach prayer. The disciples' request seemed very sincere, even desperate. He wanted to know the secret to the prayer life of Jesus.

We Need Direction

Shortly after I confessed Jesus is Lord and made Him the Lord of my life, I began to sense that I was being "called" into ministry. That is a descriptive term that we use to describe that the Holy Spirit gives a person an assignment in the Church.

> *For many are called, but few are chosen. - Matthew 22:14*

To be called means to be invited. To be chosen means to attend to the invitation. It means to show up.

As I felt this calling from the Holy Spirit, I struggled because I knew nothing about Christianity; I wasn't raised in the Church, so hearing this "calling" was something out of my ballpark. I needed to hear from God to confirm what I was sensing in my spirit.

> *The Lord directs the steps of the godly. He delights in every detail of their lives. — Psalm 37:23 (NLT)*

I laid three college portfolios on my coffee table and prayed for direction. I had my preference, but how could I know which college would be the best choice. I remember asking, "Father, I don't know what is best for my life, but I trust that you do. Please give me direction for this decision."

I was hoping to hear the voice in the coal mine, but I didn't. Although, I did sense a nudging toward the third option, which was my least favorite.

The next day, I went by the local Church to see the pastor and ask his advice. As I was waiting to go into his office, I noticed a poster on the bulletin board advertising my third option, Central Bible College. The picture on the poster showed three students, one girl, and two guys. They were the perfect examples of how young ministry students should look.

My pastor, Charles Taylor, and his wife invited me to their home after Sunday service. A guest missionary was there who had attended one of the colleges that I was considering. I took advantage and asked him, "I will be attending Bible college this next fall; I'm interested in the one that you attended. Do you recommend it?"

Expecting to get a raving endorsement, I was surprised when he said, "For you, no, I would recommend Central Bible College in Springfield, Missouri."

A few days later, my biological father called me and said, "Neil, I understand that you are a Christian now and are planning on becoming a minister. I want to help you if I can." He went on to tell me that he and his wife had moved to Branson, Missouri, just south of Springfield, to open and operate a music theatre.

After all of the circumstances, I was sure that Central Bible College would be the right choice.

I moved to Springfield. Within a few weeks of attending Bible College, the girl on the poster hanging on the bulletin board outside of my pastor's office asked me out on a date and later became my wife. Kay and I have walked in agreement together for 36-years now.

I am so glad that we can hear from God and have an intentional direction for our lives.

Prayer Can Be Taught

While attending college, I participated in a seminar, *Could You Not Tarry One Hour,* by Dr. Larry Lea. This teaching radically changed my life and laid the foundation for a lifetime of prayer.

Dr. Lea's teaching used the Lord's Prayer as the outline to pray for one hour each day. At that time, the idea of praying for one hour was radical. Most of my prayer time could be counted in minutes, not hours. We will discover later that the time we pray is not the secret sauce for effective praying, but at this early stage in my life, praying for one hour would be like running a marathon.

As daunting as this task was at first, it proved to be a tremendous help. I want to give you the outline as I have prayed it. Although I have made some adjustments through the years, I have prayed this outline for 38-years. I will use the ancient language of the King James on purpose with the hopes that we can adapt the poetry of it to the practical:

The Lord's Prayer

by Dr. Larry Lea (Revised by Neil Kennedy)

"Our Father Which Art in Heaven"

Thank God that you can call Him "Father" by virtue of the blood of Jesus.

"Hallowed Be Thy Name"

- Praise God for Who He is and for what He has done for us.
- Hallow the Names of God corresponding to the five benefits in the new covenant:
- Forgiveness of Sin; Fullness of the Spirit; Soundness in Health; Success in Life; Security in Destiny.
- In faith; declare that God is your provision in these areas:

1. Jehovah-Tsidkenu means Jehovah our righteousness.
2. Jehovah-M'kaddesh means Jehovah who sanctifies.
3. Jehovah-Shalom means Jehovah is our peace.
4. Jehovah-Shammah means Jehovah is there.
5. Jehovah-Rophe means Jehovah heals.
6. Jehovah-Jireh means Jehovah's provision shall be seen.
7. Jehovah-Nissi means Jehovah my banner.
8. Jehovah-Rohi means Jehovah, my Shepherd.

"Thy Kingdom Come, They Will Be Done"

Pray for:

- Yourself and your family (spouse, children, other members).
- Your Church (pastor, leadership, members, harvest of souls).
- Your Nation (city, state, national spiritual, and political

leaders).
- Jerusalem, Israel (Psalm 122:6)

"Give Us This Day Our Daily Bread"

- In the will of God.
- Believe it is God's will to meet your needs and prosper you to fulfill your purpose.
- Be as specific as possible.
- Be tenacious. Don't give up.

"Forgive Us Our Debts As We Forgive Our Debtors"

- Ask God to forgive you. Repent.
- Forgive and release others.
- Do not keep any bitter-morsels of unforgiveness.

"Lead Us Not Into Temptation, But Deliver Us From Evil"

Put on the whole armor of God (Ephesians 6:10-18)

1. Gird your loins with TRUTH.
2. Cover your heart with RIGHTEOUSNESS.
3. Stand firmly in PEACE.
4. Shield yourself with FAITH.
5. Protect your mind with SALVATION.
6. Firmly grasp the sword of the Spirit, the Word of God.

Pray a hedge of protection around yourself and your family (Psalm 91:2).

- Satan has no unsettled claims on your property and possessions.
- You have no open gates for the enemy to access.

"For Thine Is The Kingdom, The Power, and The Glory Forever!"

- Lift your hands in praise!
- Open your mouth and give Him thanks!
- Worship Him for His goodness and kindness!

> **ACTION STEP: We've designed a printable PDF of this outline of prayer. Please email me at ONeilKennedy@gmail.com, put in the subject line, Prayer Guide, and I will send it to you.**

A few years ago, I was in an airport in Nashville, Tennessee, making a connection to my next flight. As I walk, I try to be very attentive to people rather than consider them obstacles in my path. From a distance, I noticed a man that I recognized. It was Dr. Larry Lea. Although I had never met him before, I considered him a great friend. I immediately approached Dr. Lea introduced myself, giving him a gift of a few hundred dollars; I said, "I am indebted to you. I give thanks for you every morning when I pray because you taught me how to approach my Father."

Tears began to drip from his eyes. With a familiar smile that I recognized from years ago, he thanked me for letting him know what his teaching did for me.

Forgive Those Who Sin Against You

After this prayer outline, Jesus reiterated, "If you forgive those who sin against you, your heavenly Father will forgive you. But if you refuse to forgive others, your Father will not forgive your sins." (Matthew 6:14-15)

> *Principle: The manner in which you respond when someone calls upon you is the manner in which God responds when you call upon Him.*

It is essential to be proactive to forgive. Notice that you have the power to forgive. It is within your authority. It's a decision that you make to either hold onto or release the wrongs, hurts, pains, or evil that went against you.

Be quick to forgive.

> **Hatred stirs up contentions, but love covers all transgressions. — Proverbs 10:12**

Have you noticed when Jesus was beaten, tortured, spat upon, mocked, ridiculed, and even crucified – he still seemed in control? So much so that while antipathy rallied against Him, He made this request, *"Father, forgive them for they do not know what they are doing."*

An early follower of Jesus named Stephen was incredibly persuasive in speaking and demonstrated signs and wonders among the people. Jealous leaders stirred up contentions against him, lying about what he had said and questioning his character. During the hasty trial, Stephen was so convincing with his argument about the life and death of Jesus; haters picked up stones to murder him. As he is being martyred, he says, *"Lord, do not hold this sin against them."*

Interestingly, a young man named Saul was there at the stoning of Stephen. With his forgiveness, Stephen released this murder from Saul's record. This Saul would become Paul, the most influential Apostle in Christianity.

This is a pivotal moment with eternal ramifications. Because of Stephen's forgiveness of Saul, released Jesus to intervene and stop Saul on the road to Damascus.

> Principle: Withholding forgiveness can often hinder
> the work that God can and will do in the lives of others.

These two examples are the pinnacle of someone covering transgressions. Yet, we are often much quicker on the draw to lash out against anyone who shows us dislike. When someone treats us with disrespect, we offer our disgust immediately. If anyone trespasses upon our rights, we want to straighten them out.

I will admit, this one has been the most difficult for me. I have been pretty quick to let people know where they stand with me. I have never been accused of being passive. Sometimes my Oklahoma nature is to fight first, then ask questions. That's why I must rely on my new character in Christ.

I've seen the wisdom of covering transgressions. Both Jesus and Stephen were in control of themselves during their deaths – when hatred so moved people to kill them – they responded with forgiveness. They proved better than their adversaries. They were superior.

We are most like Christ when we cover sins.

When You Fast

When you fast, don't make it obvious, as the hypocrites do, for they try to look miserable and disheveled so people will admire them for their fasting. I tell you the truth, that is the only reward they will ever get. — Matthew 6:16

Jesus made corrections regarding fasting. Notice that Jesus didn't say, "if you fast," but He said, "when you fast."

What is fasting?

In the most straightforward answer, it means to abstain from food.

There are some excellent books on fasting. However, when it comes to fasting for spiritual purposes, we need more insight. I recommend Jentezen Franklin's book, *Fasting.* He has probably done more to inspire fasting in this generation than anyone.

Principle: If you want the awards of man, do what you do publicly. However, if you want the rewards of God, do your deeds privately.

Let me give you a few insights that have helped me when I fast.

- **Fasting is not for the novice.** It would be best if you had some spiritual maturity before fasting. I've seen many young believers shipwreck their faith because they began to fast too quickly in their walk with God.
- **When you fast, you open yourself up to the spirit realm, not just the authorized Spirit or Holy Spirit.** The first voice that Jesus heard while fasting was Satan, quoting scriptures.
- Whatever you hear during a fast should be carefully and diligently checked with scriptures. **Nothing that you hear from God will be contrary to the Word of God.**
- **Do not allow the humility of fasting to puff you up spiritually.** I've seen many people become prideful by their demonstration of humility.
- **Be private.** You negate the benefits of fasting if you parade yourself as fasting publicly.
- **Fasting without prayer is a religious diet without results.**
- Fasting does not demand God do something He does not want to do. **It aligns us with His will, not convince Him to do our will.**
- **Shut your mouth.** If you're grumbling, complaining, and gossiping during your fast, go ahead and eat because you're missing the point.

ACTION STEP: I have a fast based on Isaiah 58. Please email me at NeilKennedy@FivestarMan.com, put in the subject line, Isaiah 58 Fast, and I will send you a PDF copy of it.

3

Show Us the Father

Philip said, "Lord, show us the Father, and we will be satisfied." - John 14:8

How do you see the invisible God?

Worshippers are tempted to confine God into an image. We're tempted to be men who believe what we see rather than see what we believe. Yet, God has never allowed man to carve out His image. It is a ridiculous notion for man to think that he has the skill and craft to confine God into a carving of wood or stone. Men do it, only to their fallacy, they do it.

You have seen their detestable practices and their idols made of wood, stone, silver, and gold. - Deuteronomy

29:17

The word detestable means contaminated, polluted, filthy, something to loathe. If I were to use crass language, I would describe it as dung!

> Principle: The god that you can craft and contain with your hands is deaf, mute, blind, and worthless. Those who worship worthless idols become worthless worshippers.

It's such a foolish notion for anyone to think that the hands of contaminated man could craft the omnipotent, omniscient, omnipresent, and sovereign God.

Philip leans on the notion, "Show us the Father."

Jesus responded, "Have I been with you all this time, Philip, and yet you still don't know who I am? Anyone who has seen me has seen the Father!"

Jesus is the expressed image of the Father. The only option for a man to see a physical representation of God, the Father, is to see His Son, Jesus, in the flesh.

The Son radiates God's glory and expresses the very character of God, and he sustains everything by the mighty power of his command. When he had cleansed us from our sins, he sat down in the place of honor at the right hand of the majestic God in heaven. - Hebrews 1:3

The Son Image of His Father

When Adam was 130 years old, he became the father of a son who was just like him—in his very image. He named his son Seth. —Genesis 5:3

Adam's son, Cain, committed the first murder—a fratricide—killing Abel. Adam had another son who was the expressed image of himself, named Seth.

Seth means compensation or set in the place of another.

In the same manner, when Adam sinned against God and was no longer the shadowed image of God, made after His likeness, the Father expressed His image on His Son, Jesus.

However, the physical image of Jesus is not the attraction to Him.

My servant grew up in the Lord's presence like a tender green shoot, like a root in dry ground. There was nothing beautiful or majestic about his appearance, nothing to attract us to him. —Isaiah 53:2 (NLT)

I believe it is important to point this out because we live in a society so enamored with cuteness. As the Spirit told the

25

prophet, "Men look on the outward appearances, but God examines a man's heart." (1 Samuel 16:7)

Once again, it's an absurd notion to capture the physical image of Jesus with the brush strokes of contaminated hands.

To be transparent, I hesitate to point out because it will almost certainly offend some to think that Jesus wasn't cute like the feminized, flowing blond, European Jesus portrayed in so many paintings. The point is that Jesus was ordinary in physical appearance, yet His words, actions, attributes, and character were just like His Father. The brilliance of the Son is the perfect reflection of His Father's character.

Our encouragement from this is that you and I do not have to model ourselves in a physical appearance or have a denom-inational dress code to look like Him, but our sonship will be evident in our words, actions, and characteristics of the Father.

Jesus said, *"If you had really known me, you would know who my Father is. From now on, you do know Him and have seen Him!"*

So, if you want to see the reflection of the Father, you look to Jesus. Jesus is the way to see Him. He is the Truth, the uncontaminated version of the Father.

> *"We are not stoning you for any good work," they replied, "but for blasphemy, because you, a mere man, claim to be God." - John 10:33*

Once again, the Jewish opponents of Jesus were rabid with antipathy for Him to say, *"I and the Father are one."*

As was Jesus' custom to respond to accusatory and false charges, He referred to the authority of scripture and prophecy.

In this case, He quoted Psalm 82:6,

> *"Is it not written in your Law, 'I have said you are "gods?" If he called them 'gods,' to whom the word of God came—and Scripture cannot be set aside—what about the one whom the Father set apart as his very own and sent into the world? Why then do you accuse me of blasphemy because I said, 'I am God's Son?' Do not believe me unless I do the works of my Father. But if I do them, even though you do not believe me, believe the works, that you may know and understand that the Father is in me, and I in the Father."*

The evidence of sonship is not just what we say with our mouths but also the results that we have in our lives. People who know us should immediately hear and see the evidence of the Father's expression on us.

You Can Ask Me Anything

> *You can ask for anything in my name, and I will do it, so that the Son can bring glory to the Father. Yes, ask me for anything in my name, and I will do it! - John 13-14*

Immediately, men hesitate after hearing this powerful statement from Jesus. They are compelled to put contingencies on the idea, "anything." They feel that Jesus went a little too far with the use of that word. Did you? Do you?

When you read that promise, did you pause with a doubting thought, "anything?"

I know that I have many times. I read it then my mind begins to question or place limits on my requests. It's impossible to pray in faith while doubting.

I've known ministers who spend hours preaching and explaining away the statement suggesting that we can ask anything.

Rather than examining the unlimited potential of this promise, again, we want to craft a contaminated image of God.

Our Father will not give us evil. But I will suggest that if you're asking for something evil, you're not His Son in the first place.

> *Which of you, if your son asks for bread, will give him a stone? Or if he asks for a fish, will give him a snake? If you, then, though you are evil, know how to give good gifts to your children, how much more will your Father in heaven give good gifts to those who ask him! - Matthew 7:9-11 (NIV)*

> *Every good and perfect gift is from above, coming down from the Father of the heavenly lights, who does not change like shifting shadows. - James 1:17 (NIV)*

As contaminated as we are, we know our sons and daughters and perceive what is best for them. Our parental intuition for their future helps raise them and bless them. In the same way, our Father knows what is good and perfect for us. He won't play tricks on us. He won't change and have emotional ups and downs that determine His goodness.

You can be sure that when you ask the Father for something, He will not be stingy or cheap with His reply. He is a generous Father without limitations or resources.

But when you ask him, be sure that your faith is in God alone. Do not waver, for a person with divided loyalty is as unsettled as a wave of the sea that is blown and tossed by the wind. - James 1:6

You will never ask with confidence if you do not know the character of your Father.

The Character of Your Father

1. He is Infinite—without origin (Psalm 147:5).
2. He is Immutable—never changes (Malachi 3:6).
3. He is Self-Sufficient—lacks nothing (John 5:26).
4. He is Omnipotent—all-powerful (Psalm 33:6).
5. He is Omniscient—all-knowing (Isaiah 46:9-10).
6. He is Omnipresent—Everywhere (Jeremiah 23:23).
7. He is Wisdom—perfect in understanding and discernment (Romans 11:33).
8. He is Faithful—completely reliable, true, unwavering (2 Timothy 2:13).
9. He is Good—His kindness leads us to repent (Psalm 34:8).
10. He is Just—has perfect judgment (Deuteronomy 32:4).
11. He is Merciful—compassionate (Romans 9:15).
12. He is Gracious—lovingkindness and slow to anger (Psalm 145:8).

13. He is Love—He personally loves you (1 John 4:7-8).
14. He is Holy—infinite perfection, incorruptible (Revelation 4:8).
15. He is Glorious—indescribable and unattainable radiance (Habakkuk 3:4).

It takes time to meditate on these characteristics and attributes to grasp fully. However, if we're going to take the limits off of our ask—we must know the character of our Father. We will not have the confidence to approach Him and ask of Him if we do not know Him.

I have written this to you who believe in the name of the Son of God, so that you may know you have eternal life. And we are confident that He hears us whenever we ask for anything that pleases Him. And since we know He hears us when we make our requests, we also know that He will give us what we ask for. - John 5:13-15 (NLT)

One day my daughter, Courtney, came to me with a request, "Dad, I need a new cell phone." I answered, "No, you don't need a new one; you want a new one."

She said, "Ok, I want a new cell phone. I also know that you delight in granted the desires of my heart. I want to please you by having you get me a new cell phone."

You can imagine that she got what she asked of me.

Courtney appealed to my character as a father who delights in granting the desires of her heart. She was confident to ask me because she knew me. She knows that I want the best for her. I delight in her. I anticipate her needs and make provisions for her.

Of course, my daughter, Alexandra, and my son, Chase knew equally as well. I was no respecter of my children and sought to meet their individual needs and desires. Also, knowing that each of them was different required me to discern the individualism of their needs.

In the same way, God is no respecter of persons. He deals with each of us according to our individual needs, desires, and purposes in life.

That is why I do not need to covet what another person has received. God is not limited and will not run dry of resources. Those who covet are unbelievers. They do not know the omnipotent Father. To them, your gain is their loss.

For the believing son, when we see another person receive from God, we can rejoice with them, knowing that our Father is generous and discerning. He will meet all our needs according to His riches.

> *The Lord be exalted, who delights in the well-being of his servant.* — Psalm 35:27

As a father, I deeply desire that my children prosper. To prosper is a Biblical concept. It means so much more than money. It means that you have the means to fulfill your meaning in life. Prosperity has a purpose. Money is a tool for prosperity, not the goal of it. I raised my children with the desire to meet their needs, grant the wishes of their hearts, and help finance their purposes.

Now that my children are adults and have children of their own, I am thrilled to see them experiencing the rewards of their purposes.

If I have this fulfillment, don't you expect that our Father also enjoys this when we ask Him in faith and answering our requests helps us fulfill the purposes of our lives?

Look at the first miracle of Jesus. What did He do? He provided wine for a wedding to save the embarrassment of lack.

This act points to His character. He is kind. He is gracious. He wants to save us from embarrassment. He is also omnipotent—Jehovah-Jireh—He will provide.

Your Father Knows What You Need

And in praying do not heap up empty phrases as the Gentiles do; for they think that they will be heard for their many words. Do not be like them, for your Father knows what you need before you ask Him. —Matthew 6:7

Do you remember the contest on Mount Carmel?

A prophet, Elijah, called for a contest between himself and the 450 prophets of Baal on Mount Carmel. It was a simple request for any god to perform, two bulls laid on the altar, the wood underneath them, without setting them on fire, call on the name of your god and see who burns up the sacrifice.

The 450 prophets of Baal went first; for hours, they cried, danced, hobbled around the altar, shouted louder, cut themselves with knives and swords, but no sound from heaven, no reply from Baal, no response with fire.

Elijah mocked them. He was laughing at them. He said, "Shout louder, maybe he is daydreaming, or maybe your god is in the bathroom relieving himself. He might be on a trip, far away! Maybe you need to wake him up!"

Pull out your timer on your phone or watch and read this prayer out loud,

> *"Lord, the God of Abraham, Isaac, and Israel, let it be known today that you are God in Israel and that I am your servant and have done all these things at your command. Answer me, Lord, answer me, so these people will know that you, Lord, are God, and that you are turning their hearts back again." - 1 Kings 18:36*

It took me 20 seconds!

When Elijah prayed this prayer, fire came down from heaven and burned up the sacrifice, the wood, the stones, and the soil.

It takes a temperature of 1,100 to 2,400 degrees Fahrenheit to melt rock.

The fire from God burned up the stones of the altar!

The fire also vaporized the water instantly.

> Principle: We're not babbling pagans attempting to get the attention of God.

We've all seen it during a church service. When someone is called upon to pray, they immediately change their voice, rhythm, accent, or dialect to pray, often with Old English. They may also use God's name and titles as transitions throughout their prayer. Please don't get me wrong, many sincere people are begging for the attention of God, but this kind of prayer is often begging for the attention of men.

What good is it to sound holy but be ineffective to be heard by God?

There have been times that I have prepared for things that my children would need. However, I waited to give it to them until they asked me for their help. As a Father, I anticipated what they would need, but also they needed to ask me for my help or assistance.

> *Leave here, turn eastward and hide in the Kerith Ravine, east of the Jordan. You will drink from the brook, and I have directed the ravens to supply you with food there.* — *1 Kings 17:4*

> *Go at once to Zarepath in the region of Sidon and stay there. I have directed a widow there to supply you with food.* — *1 Kings 17:9*

What I want you to see in these two verses is that God directed the ravens and the widow to take care of the needs of Elijah.

There are times when you're walking in obedience to God's will and face difficult circumstances, as a result of the very Word of God that you are testifying; yet, God is still personal enough and caring enough to care for the details of your life.

> Principle: God knows what you need, but you need to ask Him.

Elijah was a man, just like you; he had frailties, emotions, and at times, ego. But when he prayed, he had supernatural answers to his prayers. He prayed that the skies would dry up and withhold rain — for three and a half years, it did not rain.

During the drought, he had to rely on God to meet his needs. Again, notice the word God "directed" the ravens and the widow. Amazingly, the widow certainly didn't know that she was directed until she heard Elijah ask for a small loaf of bread.

Most people would jump to the conclusion that Elijah was just another greedy preacher asking a widow for her last meal. How ruthless could he be?

People who talk like that don't know the scriptures or the principles of God. The best thing that she could ever do was to receive the prophet so that she could receive the prophet's reward.

> *Whoever welcomes a prophet as a prophet will receive a prophet's reward." — Matthew 10:41*

> Principle: The miracle process of receiving happens at the ask moment.

This is a principle that very few men fully grasp. Sometimes, we have an attitude that we must "Man Up" and be our own man—thinking that asking is a sign of weakness. When in reality, asking is a testimony of a relationship.

> *You desire but do not have, so you kill. You covet but you cannot get what you want, so you quarrel and fight. You do not have because you do not ask God. — James 4:2*

I can tell you that most people live this scripture day in and day out. What is causing all of the strife, violence, and racial divisions in our time? It is the desires that battle within us.

The word desire is best understood as pleasures or lusts. This isn't the healthy desire to do God's will and believe in God's best in your life. It is the appetite for hedonistic fulfillment which is idolatry. It's a burning fire that rages within a person, motivating them to do all kinds of evil.

James tells us that the answer to all of these problems is asking God. However, the "ask" that gets the attention of God also comes from our relationship with Him.

> *And if you ask, you won't receive it for you're asking with corrupt motives, seeking only to fulfill your own selfish desires. —James 4:3*

James calls this spiritual adultery — a spiritual affair with the world.

Most people chase after other people's stuff rather than asking God to supply their needs.

I would suggest that you can't pray a prayer of faith that is a lie. When you pray to the Father, you can't lie about your motives. He knows your thoughts and motivations. So, your prayer isn't even heard because your impurities cancel it out.

But when you do ask your Father, as a son seeking to be honorable and fulfill His will and purpose for your life, I can assure you that not only does He hear you, He will do what you ask.

> *Since we have this confidence, we can also have great boldness before him, for if we ask anything agreeable to*

> *his will, he will hear us. And if we know that he hears us in whatever we ask, we also know that we have obtained the requests we ask of him.* — 1 John 5:14

My children were never shy about asking me for something they already knew I wanted them to have what they wanted. It's pretty easy to be bold to ask when you know that your Father wants you to have and has already made provision for what you're asking.

That's why it is vital to know God's will and not rely on what other people have suggested.

Principle: Don't allow the limited beliefs of others to define your ask.

4

The Sons of God Revealed

For all who are led by the Spirit of God are sons of God.
— *Romans 8:14 (ESV)*

We have not received the spirit of slavery or fear. The Gospel, the Good News that Jesus has set us free from sin, is the most remarkable miracle known in heaven and on earth.

We have received the Spirit of adoption as sons. The depth behind this truth stretches your mind in the attempt to grasp what God has done entirely.

Adam was made in the likeness and image of God. Adam willingly disobeyed God's word. He was commanded to "multiply and fill the earth." However, Adam lost everything, including the assignment to cover the earth with the seed that he had been given in the storehouse of the Garden.

The blessing of multiplication was in the DNA — spiritually and biologically. However, after his embezzlement, the ground began to work against him. He lost access to the storehouse of seed. He also lost directional intent to fill the earth.

Adam became a nomad — a wanderer on the earth.

The Epic Battle of Seed

God spoke the first Messianic prophesy to the Satan who possessed the body of the serpent in Genesis 3:15,

> *"And I will cause hostility between you and the woman,*
> *and between your offspring and her offspring.*
> *He will strike your head,*
> *and you will strike his heel."*

Principle: We are born into an epic battle of seed.

This prophecy is speaking directly concerning the Seed (speaking of the Messiah, namely Jesus) that will strike the Head of Satan.

The Head is always representative of authority.

As a husband is the Head of his wife and family, he is responsible for protecting, promoting, prospering, and empowering them. This authority is servant leadership. It is servanthood because the Head is willing to lay down his life for his family.

However, Satan gained authority because Adam believed the lie and surrendered his place, exposing himself, figuratively discovering himself naked.

Satan's headship isn't marked by servant-leadership but by domination, which is slavery. He operates the world on the spirit of domination. Satan rebelled from God's throne. He removed himself from the protocol of authority.

Satan deceived Eve, but Adam willingly disobeyed the Word of God that he had heard. By doing so, Adam stepped out of the protocol of authority, thus exposing his entire family to the malevolent that would terrorize them.

Domination drives the elites of our day to oppress and subjugate the people they are leading. They do not have authority above them; therefore, they only have control by domination. It is not from God.

As Jesus said, *"The kings of the Gentiles lord it over them; and those who exercise authority over them call themselves Benefactors."*

You can recognize satanic leadership regardless of the venue or governmental system by seeing the benefits flow. If all of the benefits flow to the administration, it is satanic. If the representatives of people are enriched, empowered, rewarded, and excluded from the laws they impose on others, you can be assured that it is evil.

> Principle: Any leadership designed to be served rather than serve is satanic.

God gave man dominion over the earth, not domination over other men. You see one group exercising domination over others when you see satanic work.

ACTION STEP: I have written a book on the protocol of authority, The Centurion Principle. Please email me at ONeilKennedy@gmail.com, put in the subject line, Centurion Principle, and I will send you an ebook copy.

The Satanic Plot to Contaminate Humanity

In Genesis 6:2, we see the fruition of the satanic plot to dominate humanity.

> *Then the people began to multiply on the earth, and daughters were born to them. The sons of God saw the beautiful women and took any they wanted as their wives. Then the Lord said, "My Spirit will not put up with humans for such a long time, for they are only mortal flesh. In the future, their normal lifespan will be no more than 120 years."*

The term *bēn* means sons, offspring, or seed. The term, sons of God, in this verse is *bēn'ĕlōhîm*, refers to the progeny of:
   a. rulers, judges
   b. divine ones
   c. angels
   d. gods

Many speculative teaching comes out of these verses simply

because we don't have enough information. The uncanonical resource of the Book of Enoch gives insight into this verse, yet we should not build doctrine on it.

Some damnable doctrines derived from this verse are used to subjugate people, enslave people, or dehumanize people. That is an example of the satanic desire for domination. Satan will often entice false teachers, preachers, and prophets to misuse scripture for their gain and satisfy their itch.

However, we know that there is a contamination of all off-spring on the earth. David cried out, *"I was brought forth in iniquity, and in sin did my mother conceive me." (Psalm 51:5 ESV)*

We all have iniquity, perversity, and depravity that we're born with. In other words, no child is born without sin — they are conceived in it. That is why Jesus had to be born of a virgin. The seed of man was not pure. It was contaminated. The doctrine of the virgin birth is foundational to understanding the substitutionary work of Christ.

Abraham, the Father of Faith

This inherited contamination of sin and depravity is why God called Abraham to leave his native country, relatives, and father's family to a new inheritance. That is why Abraham is called the patriarch of faith. He obeyed and followed the directional intent of God.

You realize Abraham's struggle with having a promise without the potential to fulfill it. He was promised to be the father of many nations, yet his wife Sarah was barren. How could he father nations if he could not father a promised son?

However, he believed in the word of God that spoke to him. His wife, Sarah, walked in agreement with that promise. And a whole nation came from a man that was as good as dead. It was as the spirit of resurrection empowered his body.

Even more than that, Abraham is not just the father of flesh and blood, but he is the father of all men who believe by faith. We are the true sons of Abraham.

> *Know then that it is those of faith who are the sons of Abraham. And the Scriptures, foreseeing that God would justify the Gentiles by faith, preached the gospel beforehand to Abraham, saying "In you shall all the nations be blessed." So then, those who are of faith are blessed along with Abraham, the man of faith.* — Galatians 3:7-9

I love the Jewish people. I am forever grateful for them because, through the Jewish people, the Seed came and delivered all of humanity. So, in Christ, there is no distinction between Jew and Gentile.

Born of Incorruptible Seed

When you accept the substitutionary work of Christ and confess with your mouth, Jesus is Lord; you are born again. You are born of incorruptible seed!

> *Being born again, not of corruptible seed, but of incorruptible, by the Word of God, which liveth and abideth*

for ever." — *1 Peter 1:23 KJV*

Now, you are a son of God!

Stop for a moment, stand to your feet, lift your hands, and thank your Father that you are His son!

Confession of Sonship

"My confession of faith is, 'Jesus is Lord.'

I confess with my mouth what I believe in my heart,

Jesus is the Son of God.

I am born again.

I am born of God.

I am not born of corruptible seed, but incorruptible, indestructible, every-living Seed of God's Word.

I am a new creation.

I am a son of God, born, not of a husband's will or human desire, but born of God.

Old things are gone. All things are new.

I am filled with the Holy Spirit, the authorized Spirit to speak to me and through me.

Out of my belly flows Living Water, the Spirit of God.

I have the mind of Christ. It is renewed.

My mind is alert, sober, and active.

I do not forget. I cast down vain imaginations.

His thoughts are higher than my thoughts.

His ways are better than my ways.

My feet are established. My steps are ordered.

I passionately pursue the purpose of God for my life.

I live my life to the fullest.
Whatever my hand does, it prospers and is thriving.
I dictate my appetites to fuel my purposes.
My body is strong, lean, and active.
My eyes are bright.
My ears hear.
I am a son of God.
I live honorably before my Father."

I often make this confession of faith at least once a day, some-times more. I stand. I say it out loud and often.

> *He came unto his own, and his own received him not.*
> *But as many as received him, to them gave he power to*
> *become the sons of God, even to them that believe on*
> *his name: which were born, not of blood, nor of the will*
> *of the flesh, nor of the will of man, but of God.* —*John*
> *1:11-13 KJV*

You're a son of God, not because you have a bloodline of purity. You're a son of God, not because you can discipline your flesh to holiness. You're a son of God, not because you can *will* yourself to win through success, fame, or fortune.

You are a son of God because you believe in Jesus and received Him as Lord!

When we cry, "*Abba, Father,*" the Holy Spirit testifies with our spirit that we are sons of God.

> *The Spirit himself testifies with our spirit that we are*
> *God's children. Now if we are children, then we are*
> *heirs—heirs of God and co-heirs with Christ, if indeed*

> *we share in his sufferings in order that we may also share*
> *in his glory.* —Romans 8:16

We are not called sons of Jesus or children of Jesus; we are co-heirs with Christ.

> Principle: The Father gave His only begotten Son so that He could have sons.

God established the earth on the precept of Seed-time-harvest. The seed must produce after its kind (Genesis 1:1). The brilliance of God is that from the beginning, He used this precept not just to have one begotten Son but many sons and daughters.

> *"I will be a Father to you,*
> *and you will be my sons and daughters,*
> *says the Lord Almighty."* —2 Corinthians 6:18

ACTION STEP: I have written a book, The Seven Laws Which Govern Increase and Order, which I teach on The Law of Seed. Please email me at NeilKennedy@FivestarMan.com, put in the subject line, Law of Seed, and I will send you an ebook copy.

The Earth Trembles

> *For the creation was subjected to futility, not willingly, but because of him who subjected it, in hope that the creation itself will be set free from its bondage to corruption and obtain the freedom of the glory of the children of God.* — Romans 8:20

There is a kinetic relationship between Adam and the earth. Adam was given dominion over the planet. He was responsible for the earth's cultivation and care. It was his job. It was Adam's vocation which means that he was called and anointed to do it. Vocation means Divine calling.

When Adam sinned against God's Word, he subjected the earth to frustration. The world didn't choose corruption. It is constantly fighting for life to thrive regardless of the storms, fires, earthquakes, famines, and volcanic eruptions. Every season, you see the earth striving to produce. However, it is in bondage to decay.

Mankind is the steward of the earth, but we've done an inferior job of it. The ground is affected by our actions. Primarily, the earth trembles because of the sin of humanity.

> *There are three things that make the earth tremble—*
> *no, four it cannot endure:*
> *a slave who becomes a king,*
> *an overbearing fool who prospers,*
> *a bitter woman who finally gets a husband,*
> *a servant girl who supplants her mistress.* — Proverbs

30:21-23

Principle: The earth responds to the acts of men.

Secularists are using this relationship with the earth as a get-rich-quick scheme and a means to control every sector of society — corporations, citizenry, and governments. They fly their private jets to exclusive resorts, sit in their ego circles, call themselves the elites, discuss their economics, and seek domination of billions of people. They do not want the earth to be better for mankind, only for "their kind."

If we want to care for the earth, the first step is to repent of our sins and become sons of God. The earth has no way of communicating its frustration, so the language of choice is trembling, storming, and erupting! It is as a woman is birthing a child; at that moment, she is birthing pain. Within seconds of seeing the child, she forgets the pain and sees only the joy of birth.

The earth is waiting for the sons of God to be revealed.

We Groan in Frustration

Not only so, but we ourselves, who have the firstfruits of the Spirit, groan inwardly as we wait eagerly for our adoption to sonship, the redemption of our bodies. — Romans 8:23

Aren't you frustrated?

I am.

I admit it. I am not happy with what I see on the earth. I am disgusted by the depravity of humanity. Look around! It is evil and violent in this world. When you think that it can't get any worse, the news reports prove otherwise.

It's not just the violence; it is the stupidity.

I had no idea the level of stupidity could be mainstream. I could fill the pages with examples only for them to be obsolete in a matter of days for even more absurdity. The lies, the delusions, the depravity is unmatched.

There are times when I don't have the words to pray.

What do I do then?

The word groan means to pray inaudibly. When you are praying, but you don't have the words.

The Spirit Helps Us in Our Weakness

In the same way, the Spirit helps us in our weakness. We do not know what we ought to pray for, but the Spirit himself intercedes for us through wordless groans. — **Romans 8:26**

As much as we want to pray the will of God, there are times when we don't know what it is that He wants to be done. This weakness becomes a strength for us. As the prophet, Joel said, **"Let the weak say, I am strong." (Joel 3:10)**

The most powerful position of prayer that you have ever known is praying in the Holy Spirit. When you do, you will undoubtedly pray the perfect will of God — allowing the Spirit to pray through you.

Principle: You're standing between heaven's will and earth's frustration.

One of the reasons and responsibilities of being a son of God on the earth is to appropriate the will of our Father on earth as He has declared it in heaven. That's what Jesus said when He taught the disciples to pray, *"Let your will be done on earth as it is in heaven."*

When Jesus faced the agonizing decision of the cross, He prayed in the Garden of Gethsemane, *"Not my will but yours be done."*

Accepting the cup of all of humanity's wickedness, iniquity, sin, evil, depravity, and perversion, along with every sickness, disease, and death — that was no small matter. It was such agony that he sweated droplets of blood.

I've prayed in agony before but never unto the point of hematidrosis (sweating blood). It only occurs when someone is suffering from extreme levels of stress.

Living out, or at some point dying at the will of God, is not always an easy moment. Indeed, the millions of Christian martyrs know the tremendous stress of choosing Christ over this world — choosing death over life.

We may or may not ever face this level of testing, but we should undoubtedly build ourselves up in the Holy Spirit so that we can face our nemesis or any trial or temptation.

> *But you, dear friends, by building yourselves up in your most holy faith and praying in the Holy Spirit.* —Jude 1:20

My friend, you should be open to receiving the Gift of the Holy Spirit. I've prayed with thousands of men to be filled with the Holy Spirit. Frankly, I can't imagine navigating this world as a follower of Christ without this empowering experience.

> **ACTION STEP: I have a short video that I would like to send you concerning being a Spirit-Empowered Man. Please email me at ONeilKennedy@gmail.com, put in the subject line, Holy Spirit, and I will send it to you.**

All Things Working For Your Good

When you pray, allowing the Holy Spirit to pray through you according to the perfect will of your Father, extraordinary things begin to happen.

> *And we know that in all things God works for the good*

> *of those who love him, who have been called according to His purpose.* —**Romans 8:28**

I can't tell you how many times I've heard people use this scripture to justify all kinds of things, even evil things, as the will and purpose of God. No, not everything that happens is God's will. That would be called fate. We're not men of fate; we are men of faith.

If we are men of fate, we don't need to pray. Praying for something to happen would be absurd for someone who thinks that what-ever-will-be-will-be. However, when you believe that God has a will, that Satan will oppose God's will, and that you are a deciding factor involved, you will certainly be a man of prayer.

Praying in the Holy Spirit, because of our weakness of not knowing what our Father's good and perfect will might be, will cause all things to work for our good.

In other words, you can't have the promise of verse 28 without the prerequisite of verses 26 and 27.

There have often been times when I did not know what to do in raising my children. I knew them, but I didn't know everyone and everything affecting their lives. Only my reliance on the Holy Spirit helped me in my times of weakness.

There are times that you must rely on the Holy Spirit.

In your marriage, you need to be depending on the Holy Spirit to help you be and remain in agreement with one another. Trust me, the enemy hates agreement, and he will try to bring disagreement in your relationship with your wife. He may try to get a third voice to deceive one of you.

It may be a coworker, a trusted confidant, or a family member that doesn't appreciate boundaries. The enemy will try to use someone to sow seeds of discord.

You need the Holy Spirit to give you discernment.

There will be all kinds of obstacles to hinder your work and advancement in your career. There will be people who undermine you. There may be coworkers who are jealous of the favor of God in your life. You should constantly pray in the Spirit for your company, company leadership, and coworkers.

Of course, in the last few years, we've seen how desperate our nation is for prayer. We must be praying in the Spirit for our nation's leaders, decision-makers, policy managers, judges, governors, et cetera.

I am convinced that we've dropped the ball in battling COVID.

Principle: Wars are fought in the heavens before victories are won on the earth.

Conformed to the Image of His Son

For those God foreknew he also predestined to be con-formed to the image of his Son, that he might be the firstborn among many brothers and sisters. — *Romans 8:29*

As a son, we must conform to the image that we see in Jesus. Remember, Jesus is the perfect expression of His Father. We should also be recognized as a son of God.

When we walk into a room, it should be evident that we are sons of God. That is not determined by dressing in a particular denominational uniform. What is important is that we are clothed in the attributes of God. That's why the armor of God is not carnal weaponry.

> *Do not conform to the pattern of this world, but be transformed by the renewing of your mind. Then you will be able to test and approve what God's will is—his good, pleasing and perfect will.* — Romans 12:2

To conform to this world means that your mind and character, even how you fashion yourself is a copycat of this world. To be transformed is a metamorphosed experience when you take on a completely different figure.

We got a glimpse of this when Jesus was transfigured in front of some disciples. It must have been a fantastic experience for them and will be for us in the future.

Out transformation is by the renewing of our minds. Then we're able to know the will of God.

I have had to decide to move my family eight times because of God's will for our lives, specifically my ministry assignment. I have friends and family members that questioned my thought process because it seemed that I was giving up on everything that we had worked to achieve.

However, I can look back now and see the wisdom of God in those decisions. Don't get me wrong; they were tough decisions. Every move that I made cost me every dime that I had at the time.

You heard me right.

Every time my Father asked me to make a move in ministry, it cost me everything that I had worked to achieve. I emptied my bank accounts on every move.

The only way I could do that was that I had confidence that my Father knew my future better than I did.

> *"What no eye has seen,*
>   *what no ear has heard,*
>   *and what no human mind has conceived"*
>   *the things God has prepared for those who love him—*
>   *these are the things God has revealed to us by his Spirit.*
>   *The Spirit searches all things, even the deep things of God. For who knows a person's thoughts except their own spirit within them? In the same way no one knows the thoughts of God except the Spirit of God.* —1 Corinthians 2:9-11*

You can only make these kinds of life-changing decisions if you have access to the mind of God. You can only know His thoughts by prayer and the discernment of the Holy Spirit.

5

The Seven Steps in the Daily Commute

The steps of a man are established by the LORD, when he delights in his way; though he fall, he shall not be cast headlong, for the LORD upholds his hand. – Psalm 37:23-24 (ESV)

It was time for me to get a new Suburban. I had driven my 2004 GMC Yukon XL 457,000 miles. The hour meter showed that I had spent over one year of 24-hour days in that leather seat. It still looked great. I had worked hard to keep it maintained and clean. I had purchased eight sets of Michelin tires. It had a few issues. One, in particular, I've yet to live down.

My wife, Kay, traveled with me to a speaking engagement in Texas. The summer heat was an unbearable 115 degrees. The air-conditioner went out! By the time we arrived at the hotel, she was soaking wet. Now, anytime I mention Texas, she says, "It is too hot there."

After a diligent search, I found a dealership in Dallas that specialized in Suburbans. I wanted a low-mileage, clean, black Suburban. They had several to choose from. The salesman, Mike, was incredible. He asked, "Do you want to trade in your Yukon? We'll give you the best price that we can." Without the typical negotiation tactics, we were able to reach a reasonable price.

"Sure, but I know what I have," I replied. When I revealed to Mike how many miles I had put on my Yukon, he exclaimed, "What in the world do you do to drive that much?"

I was able to tell Mike about FivestarMan and what I do to encourage men. I shared with him how grateful I was for that Yukon. I said, "Mike, I've spent more time in prayer in that truck than anywhere else on earth."

He said, "Neil, the earth is about 25,000 miles in circumference. You could have encircled it about 18 times!"

> Principle: Your world is only as big as the trails you travel.

The greatest temptation in a man's life is comfort. There are a lot of men who have limited their world simply because they're not willing to travel new trails. Their path is the same path they've always beaten. It's easy to get in a rut and stay there. It's difficult to cut a new swath.

As I mentioned earlier in this book, I was working in a coal mine when I decided to leave everything and go to college. It was hard. I had to quit my job, sell my possessions, pack my suitcase and move to another state. It wasn't easy, but it was necessary.

As I drove away from everything I was comfortable with, I prayed to God.

During that drive, I began to discover that our Father relates to men in the daily commute.

I realized that my steps had directional intent—an overwhelming realization that my Father had a destination in mind. This revelation encouraged me that God would be very involved in my decisions. Along with this new understanding came the personal responsibility to seek Him for guidance. Some call it providence, while others call it destiny. This lesson has been precious and has given me the self-assurance that I am in step with Him.

7 Steps For The Daily Commute with God

1. Spend time with God in the cool of the day.

> *And they heard the sound of the LORD God walking in the garden in the cool of the day, and the man and his wife hid themselves from the presence of the LORD God among the trees of the garden. – Genesis 3:8 (ESV)*

It had become a habit for Adam to walk with God in the cool of the day. We do not have sufficient evidence to determine how long Adam and Eve lived in daily communion with God before the horrific events of the fall. We know his decision on that day would have a global and generational impact upon mankind.

Not only was Adam expelled from his management of the Garden—the Storehouse of Seed, of which he was to "cover the earth" with the vegetation—he was also cut off from his daily commute with God.

He lost everything—his wife's trust, the respect of his chil-

dren, his home, his income, and most importantly, his relationship with his Father.

Interestingly, the day begins in the evening—when three stars
are visible. The creation account always points to the evening
and morning of the day. The cool of the day is referencing the
evening when the sun's heat has gone down.

> Principle: When you're driving home from work, leave
> the radio off and ask God to prepare you for your
> responsibility as a husband and a father to be a blessing
> to your family.

As a husband, your words are like seeds sown for a determined
harvest. Ask God to give you the right words to speak over your
wife. You don't know what her day may have been like, but the
Holy Spirit does, and He will help you have the right words—the
best words—to speak to her.

As Solomon advised, "Everyone enjoys a fitting reply;
it is wonderful to say the right thing at the right time!"
(Proverbs 15:23 ESV)

Before you turn on the evening news, get the information in
your world. Rather than coming in and plopping down on the
sofa, ask God to strengthen you so that you can go into the house
with energy and excitement to be with your family. That's what
matters most at home.

2. Determine that you will commute with God 365 days of the year.

> *Thus all the days of Enoch were 365 years. Enoch walked with God, and he was not, for God took him. – Genesis 5:23*

I am very intrigued by the great-grandfather of Noah, namely Enoch. Although he was a prophet, we have very little evidence of his life in our canonized Bible, although most Christian historians and theologians recognize his importance. Jude references him,

> *"Enoch, who lived in the seventh generation after Adam, prophesied about these people. He said, "Listen! The Lord is coming with countless thousands of his holy ones..." (Jude 1:14).*

What we can see is that he invested 365 years walking with God. The writer of Hebrews lists Enoch in the Hall of Faith,

> *"By faith Enoch was taken up so that he should not see death, and he was not found, because God had taken him. Now before he was taken he was commended as having pleased God." (Hebrews 11:5 ESV)*

Enoch walked so closely with God that he didn't experience death. He was the first person to experience what we would refer to as the rapture, the snatching away.

I've determined that I want to invest 365 days of each year walking with God. I don't want to miss a day. I don't want to wander or roam without directional intent.

3. Walking with God in the daily commute will give you promptings of future events.

> *This is the account of Noah and his family. Noah was a righteous man, the only blameless person living on earth at the time, and he walked in close fellowship with God. – Genesis 6:9*

As Noah walked closely in communion with God—in the daily commute—he discovered that a great deluge, a water baptism of the earth, was going to occur. The rest of humanity had given their hearts over to wickedness and violence. This cleansing was required to remove this scourge from the earth. However, with this warning of things to come, Noah was given the blueprints of a large ship. Noah's motivation is clear—he built the ark to save his family members.

> Principle: When you walk with your Father, He will reveal things about your future.

Many people have the erroneous idea that Noah was a radical environmentalist and animal rights activist. We should be diligent stewards of the earth's resources, and Solomon said that righteous men are kind to their animals, but Noah had one thing in mind when he spent decades building the ark—he wanted to save his family.

As you have a daily commute with God, you begin to think long-term. You'll see further into the future. Your decisions will be more accurate for things to come. As the family's progenitor, your responsibility will take on a keen sense of destiny.

4. Trust that God knows where you need to be to receive His best for you.

> *It was by faith that Abraham obeyed when God called him to leave home and go to another land that God would give him as his inheritance. He went without knowing where he was going.* – **Hebrews 11:8 NLT**

Abraham was given directional intent, even though while he was traveling, he didn't know where he would end up. He did know there would be an inheritance awaiting him upon his arrival. He had to trust the Voice he was hearing. He had to have confidence that he was hearing from God.

Principle: God can give you direction without you knowing the destination.

Sometimes I meet men who don't want to let go of their plans. They've schemed up a good idea of what they think would be best for their lives and their families.

However, I've learned that my schemes are not as good as God's dreams for me. He has a greater capacity for imagination than I do. His ways are much higher than my ways. His thoughts are much greater than my thoughts. That is probably one of the greatest challenges for men, to yield their lives and the lives of their family members to the purpose of God above our plans for ourselves or our family members.

I've learned that my schemes are not as good as God's dreams for me.

I've had to do that with my children. Now that they're grown, I've had to sit back and watch God lead them in different directions. Sometimes, I want to raise my voice and say, "Are you serious? Do you think this is a good idea?" Yet, I must allow them to develop an ear to hear the directional intent that God has for them.

Abraham had to "leave his father and his family household" to go to the inheritance that God had for him.

5. A typical day at work can become an encounter with God.

"Do not come any closer," the LORD warned. "Take off your sandals, for you are standing on holy ground.

Moses was very well educated and influential in speaking (Acts 7:22). He had a strong sense of leadership and justice; however, his first attempt to exercise leadership backfired. Now, exiled from Egypt and led into a wilderness, he had become a shepherd managing Jethro, his father-in-law's sheep.

During a typical day of work, Moses sees the burning bush that is not being consumed by the fire. As he approached to investigate the phenomenon, he encountered God.

Some men don't realize how involved God is in their work.

Principle: Turn your daily commute into communion.

Ask God to strengthen your hands to prosper. Commit that whatever your hand finds to do, you will do it with strength and skill. As you're driving to work, leave the radio off and have a daily commute with God.

Ask God to bless your company. Ask God to give you ideas and witty inventions. Commit to God that you consider your work as meaningful, not trivial. God made you a cultivator. Whatever you touch should be better after you've handled it.

6. When you're facing your greatest challenges, it's important that you walk with God.

> *Even though I walk through the valley of the shadow of death,*
> *I will fear no evil,*
> *for you are with me;*
> *your rod and your staff,*
> *they comfort me.*

When David was a young man, he attended to his father's sheep. He spent nights under the stars strumming his guitar and singing Messianic songs. During those intimate and isolated times, David had to learn to "fear no evil." During those nights, he wrestled a lion and a bear, protecting the sheep from predators. He would later take those lessons to the valley of Elah (Valley of Oak Tree), where he would face the champion, Goliath.

Facing Goliath, David recalled his past experiences of victory over the lion and the bear. He also remembered the anointing that flowed upon his young head when the prophet spoke over him that he would become a king.

> Principle: When you're facing a big-time problem, you
> can know that God is walking in this valley with you.

When you have a daily commute with God, you will remember the steps that God has guided you through. You will also be reminded of the important words of promise that you've received. They may seem small now, but they were important lessons to learn at the time.

7. Jesus descended so that he could walk with man.

He said, "Come." So Peter got out of the boat and walked
on the water and came to Jesus. Matthew 14:29

Peter and the other disciples had worked for hours, rowing to get across the lake. A storm was opposing all of their efforts. They were getting nowhere. As tired as they were, they look over to see Jesus walking on water during the storm, making more progress than they've made all night!

Sometimes we read these accounts as if they're fairy tales, yet this happened. You can imagine how frustrating it would have been to have worked all night trying to get somewhere, only to see Jesus passing you by without hardly an effort.

> Principle: Jesus descended to make eye contact with
> you so that you can ascend to make contact with your
> Father.

Jesus is God with us. He walked with men. He still walks with men.

> *Yet God sent us his Son in human form to identify with human weakness. Clothed with humanity, God's Son gave his body to be the sin-offering so that God could once and for all condemn the guilt and power of sin.* –
> *Romans 8:3*

Maybe that hits close to home for you. Your life may be at the place where you're tired of the opposition. You may have reached your limit, and you're just frustrated with the lack of progress. You may feel weak with your humanity. You may be overwhelmed with guilt and condemned by the power of sin.

You may be so ready to make progress that you're willing to take steps you've never tried before. That's what Peter did.

When Peter saw the progress Jesus was making compared to the lack of progress all his co-laborers were experiencing, Peter said, "*Hey, if it's you, Jesus, invite me to walk with you (my paraphrase).*"

Jesus came to this earth to walk with man in the daily commute. Jesus' response to Peter was, "Come." In other words, get out of the boat!

When you walk with Jesus, you can be sure to get to your destination. Of course, that is if you keep walking in faith.

So, get out of the boat and take a step of faith.

Rules for Walking on Water

1. You can't walk where you don't put your foot.
2. Don't listen to those who stay in the boat.
3. Don't consider the waves. They don't matter.
4. Keep your eyes on Jesus; He is the one who called you out of the boat.
5. If you sink, ask for help.

Remember, your world is only as big as the trails that you're willing to travel.

ACTION STEP: We've created a resource to help you navigate your daily commute with God; The Daily Champion. It is a 365-day word of encouragement that will help transform your daily commute into communion. Sign up at TheDailyChampion.com

CPSIA information can be obtained
at www.ICGtesting.com
Printed in the USA
LVHW050421170422
716164LV00007B/25